Filming in the Wild

Contents

Welcome	2
Mission 1 – Tigers	3
Mission 2 – Gorillas	8
Mission 3 – Driver ants	12
Mission 4 – Sharks	16
Mission 5 – Polar bears	20
Mission 6 – Snow leopards	24
Glossary	28
Index	29
Mission summary	30

Written by Justin Anderson

Collins

Welcome

Imagine you have been set a series of missions to make your own wildlife film. On these missions, you'll learn about the latest camera technology, how to stay safe around dangerous predators and how not to disturb the animals you are filming.

Things won't always go according to plan, but, if you're lucky, you'll get closer to amazing wildlife than you ever imagined.

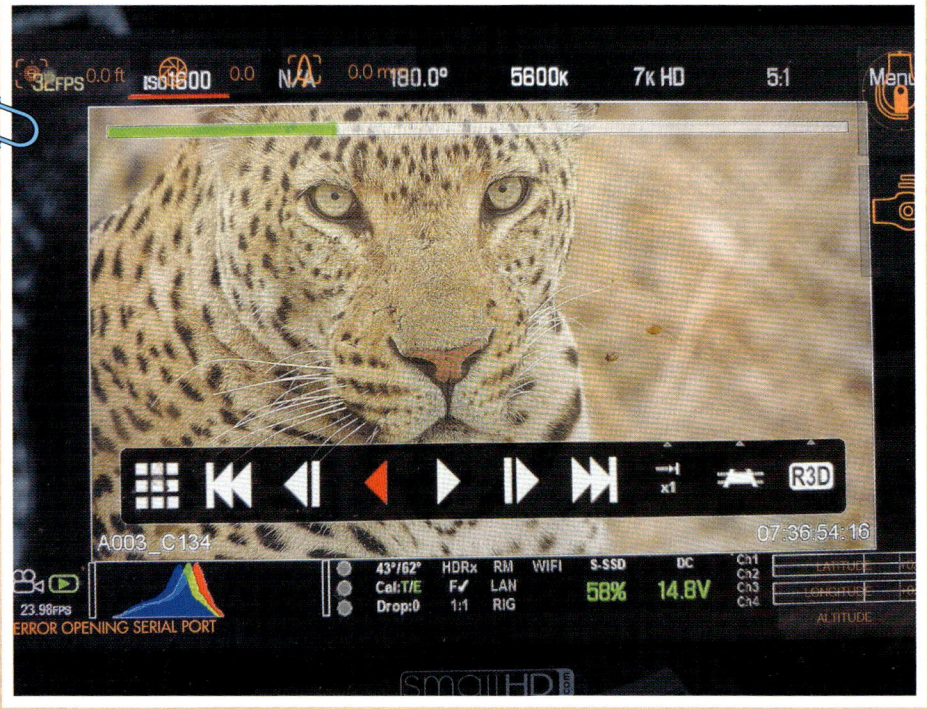

Mission 1 : Tigers

To film a tigress (a female tiger) looking after her cubs

Location: Ranthambore, India, South Asia

Difficulty:

A tigress has given birth to three small cubs in a cave in the Indian jungle. Big cats are very protective of their cubs and you need to be careful.

The challenges

Working in a hide

You'll have to sit quietly in a filming hide – a small tent, which has been **camouflaged** with leaves and branches from the forest. Remaining hidden means the tigress cannot see you, so you don't disturb her when she is tending to her cubs. You will have to sit very still and make no sound. It can take many hours, so you have to be patient. You can't even stand up, so it can be very uncomfortable.

Avoiding detection

Tigers have a strong sense of smell, so it's vital that the tigress can't smell you. Don't wash with smelly soap and be sure to rub yourself in leaves and dirt to smell like the forest.

Success! After two weeks of sitting in the hide, you capture five minutes of close-up footage showing this secretive tiger family.

Mission 2 : Gorillas

To get close-up shots of a male silverback gorilla guarding his family while they are feeding

Location: Volcanoes National Park, Rwanda, Africa

Difficulty: 6 10

Mountain gorillas live in family groups led by a **dominant** male called a 'silverback'. Gorillas are gentle and intelligent, but getting close-up shots of them isn't easy.

The challenges

Finding the gorillas

Gorillas live in the thick forests that grow on the steep sides of volcanoes, so it can
be exhausting carrying your filming equipment up the slopes.

Staying safe

Don't look the silverback directly in the eye as he will see that as a challenge. If you pretend to eat the forest plants and make low grunts like a gorilla, you can reassure the silverback that you are not a threat. If you are quiet and sit still, the gorillas may even come to you.

Not reacting

Mountain gorillas are vegetarians and their diet means they sometimes have loud rumbling tummies. But remember, you have to stay quiet!

Well done. You manage to stay quiet enough that the silverback accepts your presence and you get close enough to film the silverback gorilla.

Mission 3 : Driver ants

To film raiding driver ants to show how they hunt

Location: Nairobi, Kenya, East Africa

Difficulty:

Driver (or 'army') ants can live in **colonies** of up to 20 million! They are hunters and regularly spread out across the forest floor on a 'raid' to catch other insects and even small animals like lizards.

The challenges

Getting close

With thousands of ants, each armed with razor-sharp jaws, getting close enough to film them can be a very painful experience.

Using the right equipment

Many of the ants are only one centimetre long, so the only way to get up close to such small creatures is to use a special camera **lens** called a 'macro' lens, which acts like a magnifying glass, making small creatures appear much bigger.

Wearing long socks

The best way to avoid being bitten by driver ants is to wear thick clothes and to tuck your trousers into your socks so the ants can't crawl up your legs. But it's impossible to stop them all!

Bad luck. Heavy rain means the ants stop their raiding and there is a risk that all your camera kit will get wet and stop working. You must head home.

Mission 4 : Sharks

To dive with great white sharks and record their secret signals

Location: Guadalupe Island, Mexico, North America

Difficulty: 8 10

In the waters off the coast of Mexico lives one of the ocean's fiercest predators, the great white shark. When these sharks come together, they seem to send signals to each other by moving their fins.

The challenges

Planning carefully

Filming underwater takes lots of careful planning and a big team. You'll need a boat to live on and experienced divers to help keep you safe.

Keeping watch

Sometimes curious sharks approach you from behind. You should always dive with a 'buddy' – another experienced diver who can watch your back while you are busy filming.

Using a cage

If the sharks you find are really big, it is safer to film them from inside a protective cage made of strong metal.

Bad luck. The waterproof box for the camera has a crack in it and fills with water. Your camera stops working and you have to try and fix it on the boat. When you dive again, the sharks have gone!

Mission 5 : Polar bears

To venture far north to film how polar bears are struggling to survive a changing climate

Location: Svalbard, Norwegian Arctic, Europe

Difficulty: 9 10

The polar bear's Arctic home is so cold that each winter the surface of the ocean freezes solid. The bears like to walk out on this ice to hunt for seals but, with a changing climate, this ice is getting thinner and that can make life hard for polar bears.

The challenges

Keeping warm

You will face temperatures as low as −40° Celsius. When it's this cold, everything freezes and you have to keep the camera in its own heated jacket. It's important that you wear lots of warm clothing, too.

Following the signs

Finding polar bears in the huge expanse of frozen sea ice isn't easy. The best place to look is where big glaciers meet the sea. The bears come here to hunt for seals. If you follow the bears' pawprints, you'll soon find them.

You've done it! You manage to follow a polar bear as it struggles to walk on the thin ice – a powerful image that will show how polar bears are in trouble due to climate change.

Mission 6 : Snow leopards

To film the rare and elusive snow leopard

Location: Ladakh, India, South Asia

Difficulty: 10 10

Snow leopards are one of the hardest of all animals to film. They live high up in the peaks of the Himalaya, the tallest mountain range on Earth.

The challenges

Getting to the animals

Up in the mountains it's extremely tiring just to move around. You have to carry all the heavy filming equipment in backpacks.

Using the right camera

The only way to get close to snow leopards is to use a 'camera trap'. This small camera fits inside a plastic box and has a glass window on the front to film through. You set the traps at spots where you hope snow leopards might pass by. If they do, a signal is sent to the camera traps to start recording. It means you can film wildlife without even being there.

Missing out

The animals don't always stand in the right place to get a good shot. Sometimes your shots come back and all you have is a picture of the snow leopard's bottom!

Congratulations! You have managed to film remote shots of the rare and elusive snow leopard.

Your filming is now finished. It's time to head home and edit your shots into one film.

Glossary

camouflaged — something that is hidden or disguised so it blends in with its surroundings

colonies — groups of ants that live and work together

dominant — when individual animals are seen as more important and often make decisions for the rest of the group

lens — a curved piece of glass or plastic, used in cameras, that can make objects seem closer, larger or smaller

Index

Arctic 20

big cats 3

camera 2, 14–15, 19, 21, 26

camera trap 26

close-up 7, 8

driver ants 12–15

forest 4–5, 8–9, 12

gorillas 8–11

great white sharks 16–19

hide 4, 7

macro lens 14

polar bears 20–23

seals 20, 22

snow leopards 24–27

the Himalaya 24

tigers 3–7

Mission summary

Mission 1 : Tigers
The challenges
- working in a hide
- avoiding detection

Mission 2 : Gorillas
The challenges
- finding the gorillas
- staying safe
- not reacting

Mission 3 : Driver ants
The challenges
- getting close
- using the right equipment
- wearing long socks

Mission 4 : Great white sharks
The challenges
- planning carefully
- keeping watch
- using a cage

Mission 5 : Polar bears
The challenges
- keeping warm
- following the signs

Mission 6 : Snow leopards
The challenges
- getting to the animals
- using the right camera
- missing out

Ideas for reading

Written by Gill Matthews
Primary Literacy Consultant

Reading objectives:
- discuss the sequence of events in books and how items of information are related
- be introduced to non-fiction books that are structured in different ways
- answer and ask questions

Spoken language objectives:
- participate in discussions, presentations, performances, role play, improvisations and debates

Curriculum links: Science: Living things and their habitats

Interest words: detection, reacting, signs, watch

Word count: 1740

Build a context for reading

- Ask children to look at the front cover of the book and to read the title. Discuss what they think the book might be about and what the diver is doing.
- Read the back cover blurb and explore whether the children would like to be a filmmaker, and what they think might be involved with this job.
- Point out that this is an information book. Ask what features non-fiction books often have. Give children time to skim the book, looking for these features.

Understand and apply reading strategies

- Ask children to use the contents page to find the section called *Welcome*.
- Read p2 aloud. Demonstrate how to summarise what the book is about.